Tikiri Goes To Kinder

Written by Dr Kathy Mendis
Illustrated by Kennan Mendis

First published in 2023 through We Inspire Now Books, a business assisting authors to self-publish.

Copyright © 2023 Kathy Mendis
ISBN Paperback: 978-0-6487645-7-1

This book is copyright. Apart from any use permitted under the Copyright Act 1968, no part of this book may be reproduced, stored in or introduced into a retrieval system, or transmitted in any form, or by any means (electronic, mechanical, photocopying, recording or otherwise) without the prior written permission of the author. Any person who commits any unauthorised act in relation to this publication may be liable to criminal prosecution and civil claims for damages.
Enquiries should be made through We Inspire Now Books.

Author: Kathy Mendis
Illustrator: Kennan Mendis
Layout: Antoinette Pellegrini, We Inspire Now Books

We Inspire Now Books
PO BOX 133 Greensborough,
Victoria, Australia 3088
www.weinspirenowbooks.com

Dedication

To Peter, Brian and Kennan,
who remind me everyday of the
joy of motherhood.

Tikiri Goes To Kinder

Written by Dr Kathy Mendis
Illustrated by Kennan Mendis

Today is Tikiri's first day at kinder. Tikiri feels scared without her mama being there.

Even though her mama said, "Tikiri, you will be fine at kinder," Tikiri is not sure of this.

Most of the kids in the room don't look like Tikiri. Even the teacher looks different.

Tikiri doesn't understand what they are all saying, although she knows they are speaking in English.

Tikiri only catches a few words here and there. The words that papa taught her.

The other kids are all talking to each other. Tikiri feels a bit lonely.

Tikiri looks around the room. She sees a few other kids who also look different but they don't look like her either.

She remembers her mama saying there are many different people in the world, but they are all equal.

Tikiri remembers everyone looked the same where they lived before. She got on a plane with her mama and papa and came to Australia.

She misses her grandma and grandpa who still live over there. Tikiri starts to cry.

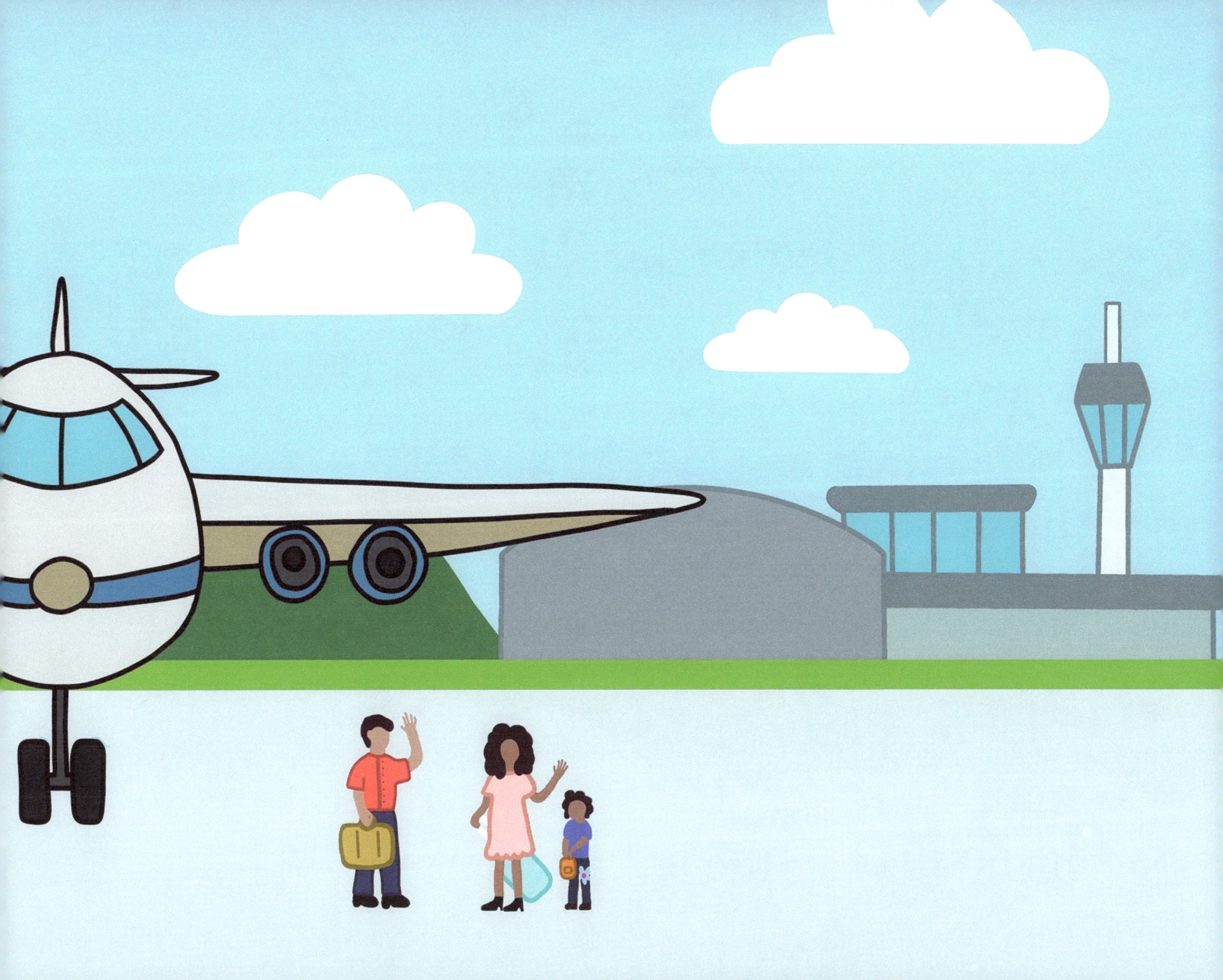

Tikiri sees the teacher is coming to her. The teacher kneels down beside Tikiri. She holds Tikiri's hand and says something but all Tikiri could do is to say, "Mama, Mama."

The teacher takes Tikiri's hand and walks with her to the bookshelf. The teacher then chooses a book and walks to her chair, still holding Tikiri's hand. She sits Tikiri in a small chair next to hers. Tikiri feels safe sitting next to the teacher.

The teacher asks everyone to come and sit in front of her and Tikiri on the floor mat.

She looks at Tikiri, nods at the book and smiles.

The teacher then opens the book and shows everyone the flag of the country where Tikiri has lived before.

Tikiri recognises some of the words the teacher is saying – names of food Tikiri usually eats, where her family goes to worship, and the names of the clothing her mama and papa usually wear.

The other kids seem excited and ask lots of questions. Tikiri feels proud because she knows the teacher is telling the other children about her country.

The teacher finishes with saying things like, "welcome" and "diverse" and "equal" and "respect". Tikiri knows what they mean because her papa has already explained them to her.

The other kids now want to be friends with Tikiri.

Some ask if they could sit next to her. Others ask if she would like to play with them.

Tikiri realises she can sort of understand what other kids are saying by looking at their faces and their moving hands.

She feels better. She knows she will soon learn how to communicate with them.

Tikiri now knows her mama is right, she is going to be fine. She feels happy.

She knows she will make friends and will enjoy kinder.

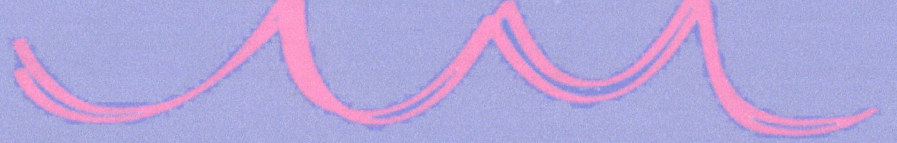

The Author
Kathy Mendis

Dr Kathy Mendis (BSW, MSW, PhD) is a social work academic who is currently working as a senior lecturer. As well as teaching in academia, she also has experience working in family violence, child protection, homelessness, family services and community development sectors and conducting academic research.

Kathy's work in providing training and consultations to kindergarten teachers and early educators about social, emotional, and behavioural impacts on children who experience trauma has inspired her to write this children's book. The idea was conceived during her visits to kindergartens when she's observed migrant children playing on their own due to communication barrier.

Kathy believes this book will help teachers and parents of pre-schoolers alike with which to explain about diversity and respect to their children at children's maturity level as well as ways in which for teachers to manage such situations.

The Illustrator
Kennan Mendis

Kennan Mendis is a visual artist based in Melbourne specialising in acrylic painting, street art and murals.

Kennan started sharing his paintings under the moniker 'Kenzopaints' in 2020, unsure of how his art would be received and his ability as a self-taught artist. To his surprise, his artworks were embraced by the Melbourne community for their quirky figures and bright patterns.

He has enjoyed exhibiting works in a number of exhibitions in Melbourne and the Surf Coast.

You can find Kennan sharing his artworks on Instagram and TikTok @kenzopaints. He also completes commissions.

You can get in touch with him at kenzopaints@gmail.com

www.ingramcontent.com/pod-product-compliance
Lightning Source LLC
Chambersburg PA
CBHW050853010526
44107CB00047BA/1600